the devil goes to church

prayer as spiritual warfare

david butts

COVENANT PUBLISHING

All Scripture quotations, unless otherwise indicated, are taken from the
HOLY BIBLE: NEW INTERNATIONAL VERSION®. NIV®. Copyright ©
1973, 1978, 1984 by International Bible Society. Used by permission of
Zondervan Publishing House. All rights reserved.

www.covenantpublishing.com

P.O. Box 390 Webb City, Missouri 64870
Call toll free at 877.673.1015

Library of Congress Cataloging-in-Publication Data

Butts, David.
    The devil goes to church : prayer as spiritual warfare / David Butts.
        p. cm.
Includes bibliographical references.
    ISBN 1-892435-34-9 (hardcover)
    1. Spiritual warfare. 2. Prayer—Christianity. I. Title.
    BV4509.5.B884 2003
    235'.4–dc21
                                    2003014055

acknowledgments

God has used so many people to contribute in so many ways to the writing and completion of this book that it is impossible to name them all. Though I will name and thank some here, I realize that ultimately this book is a project that comes from God. My prayer is that the Lord will use this material to draw many near to Him and to walk in the victory provided by Jesus.

It is always the family who bears the brunt of any writing project and mine has been no exception. My wife, Kim, has always been a great encouragement to me, even while she was in the midst of writing her first book. She always serves as my "first editor," before anyone else gets a chance to go to work on what I have written. For that and so much more, I am grateful. My grown sons, David and Ron, have encouraged me in this project and seem to like the idea of "Dad" being a writer.

Our great staff at Harvest Prayer Ministries deserves much thanks for picking up the slack when I was busy writing. The HPM staff really has become a family and we are learning to depend upon and trust one another as a family. Special thanks goes to former intern, Josh Peigh, for the great research he did specifically for this book. You were a wonderful help, Josh.

Steve Cable of Covenant Publishing had the vision to grab hold of this book idea and to encourage me to get it into print. One of the best things Steve did was to assign me John Hunter as my editor. John is a writer's dream. When things got slow in the writing, he told me to quit worrying about details and technical matters. He explained that I just need-

---

ed to let the ideas flow and put words on paper. He would come along later and clean up my mess. Thanks John!

I can't close out this section without giving special thanks to my Mom and Dad. They brought me up in the ways of God and encouraged me to follow Him always. They both saw the beginning of this work, but much has changed during the writing. Mom experienced a disabling stroke in 1997 and is living with my sister, Marianne and her family. Dad lost a battle with cancer in 1998, but in the process won the ultimate prize of eternity with Christ. I dedicate this book to them.

Dave Butts has done a wonderful service to God's people—he is addressing a most significant truth from across God's Word, and sharing it in clear and simple ways, so even a child could understand it. This is the way it should always be!

I would like to add a few thoughts to undergird what he has so adequately written. First, any truth given to His people by God must always be seen from God's perspective! And we are not ignorant about what God has revealed. His Word contains His heart and thoughts, and the Holy Spirit is our Teacher, guiding us into all truth (John 16:13). So every believer, and every church must:

- *know* the truth God has given us—primarily in His Word
- *believe* Him when He reveals truth in His Word
- *appropriate* (receive into our hearts and lives)—Him and His victory and *live* by every Word from the mouth of God (Deuteronomy 8:3). He must live out His life in each of us, and in our churches
- *live* all of life "in Christ," for He *is* our victory

Now the simple and clear truth—from the Word of God:

1. God *has already* defeated Satan, and his host, and placed them all "under the feet of Jesus" (Ephesians 1:15-23). Paul prayed that *". . . the God of our Lord Jesus Christ, the Father of glory, may give to you a spirit of wisdom and* of revelation in the knowledge of Him. I pray that the *eyes of your heart may be enlightened, so that you will know what is the hope of His calling, what are*

the riches of the glory of His inheritance in the saints," and ". . . what is the surpassing greatness of His power toward us who believe. These are in accordance with the working of the strength of His might which He brought about in Christ, when He raised Him from the dead and seated Him at His right hand in the heavenly places, far above all rule and authority and power and dominion, and every name that is named, not only in this age but also in the one to come. And He put all things in subjection under His feet, and gave Him as head over all things to the church, which is; His body, the fullness of Him who fills all in all" (NASBU). Satan, and all his hosts have been defeated, and God's people now live under this freedom God has provided (see also Colossians 2:15).*

2. We now live *from* God's victory in Christ, not *toward* victory. Remember how God provided for His people in the Old Testament. He always announced victory, as *already provided and assured by God*. His people then went out into battle (the announced victory did not mean His people did not face the enemy and have to do battle). They always fought *from* victory into the reality of the victory. This is what we do also. We still put on God's provided armor, and take our stand against the enemy, but always from victory. Paul could rightly say confidently, ". . . *thanks be to God, who always leads us in triumph in Christ. . . .*" (2 Corinthians 2:14 NASBU). It is obvious that this is how Jesus always lived, even in the presence of "the enemy." He simply announced His faith in the Father, and quoted Him from Scriptures. The enemy then "left Him," and fled.

3. Paul encouraged this Ephesian group of believers, there-fore, to *"be strong in the **Lord**, and in His mighty power. . . ."* (Ephesians 6:10). He also added, that God Himself has provided for them personally, and as a church fami-ly, His armor. We are to put on what God has provided. Dave shares this clearly and helpfully in this work.

4. One further thought, from the life of Jesus with His disci-ples. As He approached His cross, He knew every one of His disciples would be tested. Then He speaks to Peter about Satan making a request to *"sift you like wheat. . . ."* (Luke 22:31,32). Obviously this request was granted. But Jesus went on to assure Peter of God's provided victory, and what it would do in Peter. Jesus assured Peter, *". . . but I have prayed for you, that your faith may not fail; and you, when once you have turned again, strengthen your brothers. . . ."* (NASBU). What an insight into Satan's ploys, and God's provided victory. Peter would not fail, but Satan can only go so far. When that point is reached, Peter would return to Jesus—and would then, through this experience, be able to strengthen other fellow believers. And this Peter did, for the rest of his life.

5. All the strategies of Satan will not prevail—in the life of the Christian who knows God, believes Him, appropri-ates His victory in every situation and bears witness to others of God's faithfulness. This process will always bring glory to God (that is, show clearly before a watch-ing world the goodness, and greatness of God).

So, let me encourage you *as* you read and study the Scriptures in this study:

- keep it clear and simp1e
- keep all the *truth*—from God's Word, regardless of all the other "thoughts you may receive from others"
- keep it all under the teaching ministry of the Holy Spirit. Seek His guidance. Look carefully for His teaching you truth from God's Word. And obey immediately all you personally, and together hear from Him
- believe, obey and behave accordingly—and you will glorify Him. Enjoy your much-needed study! I myself have been greatly helped!

—Henry T. Blackaby
May 21, 2003

table of contents

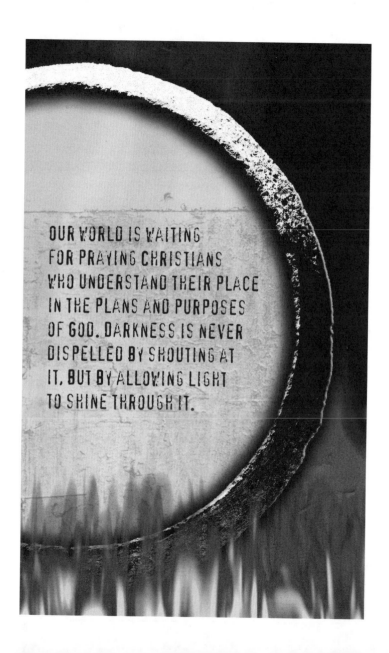

OUR WORLD IS WAITING
FOR PRAYING CHRISTIANS
WHO UNDERSTAND THEIR PLACE
IN THE PLANS AND PURPOSES
OF GOD. DARKNESS IS NEVER
DISPELLED BY SHOUTING AT
IT, BUT BY ALLOWING LIGHT
TO SHINE THROUGH IT.

*I really didn't want to write a book
about spiritual warfare!*

In the early 1990s the Lord called me from the local pastorate into a ministry of prayer and prayer mobilization. My wife, Kim, and I began a ministry called Harvest Prayer Ministries and focused on calling and equipping churches to become houses of prayer for all nations. One of a number of things that surprised us as we traveled among churches was that, in virtually every teaching session, the issue of spiritual warfare came up.

I began to put together seminars that approached prayer from the standpoint of spiritual warfare. They were well received and seemed to indicate a real need for growth in this critical area. As friends began to encourage me to write on this topic I saw a need for a very simple, small book that could be used by small groups and Sunday school classes to study this important area of a Christian's life.

There are some great books on spiritual warfare already in print and I have greatly profited in my own life from studying them. Some are listed at the end of this book. What I was hoping to do was to introduce the topic in a non-threatening, yet practical way for believers. Those desiring to go deeper in this area can use the Suggested Reading List to further their study.

This should have been a simple, easy book to write—one that was finished within a few months of its inception. But remember, it is a book on spiritual warfare. And I experienced war as I wrote it. I first sensed that I was to write this book in 1995. Now, eight years later, I'm writing the finishing touches on this short manuscript.

During those eight years, my father lost his battle with cancer and went to be with the Lord, my mother experienced a crippling stroke, and I had surgery to remove some serious cancer. The physical problems are probably just the tip of the iceberg. I certainly haven't spent eight years working on this . . . much of that time I simply laid the manuscript aside and went on to other things. Spiritual warfare is not a topic to be played with. It is a serious matter.

I can tell you that during this period of more intense warfare I have come to a greater reliance upon the Lord than ever before. Any balanced study on spiritual warfare ought to draw us nearer to the Lord. My prayer for you as you study this topic is that you will experience the Lord's presence and overcoming power in a fresh new way.

In one of my favorite books, *The Sacred Romance*, authors John Eldredge and Brent Curtis explain,

> Satan's desire is to keep us away from communion with God. He doesn't care how he does it. God's intention, on the other hand, is to use spiritual warfare to draw us into deeper communion with himself. Satan's device is to isolate us and wear us out obsessing about what he has done and what he will do next. God desires to use the enemy's attacks to remove the obstacles between ourselves and him, to reestablish our dependency on him as his sons and daughters in a much deeper way. Once we understand that, the warfare we are in begins to feel totally different. It is not really even about Satan anymore,

but about communion with God and abiding in Jesus as the source of life. The whole experience begins to feel more like a devotional (p. 120).

My desire is that Christians studying this book would begin to pray differently as a result of seeing the reality of our current warfare. When we speak of spiritual warfare, we are not so much focusing on that which is weird or strange, as we are simply facing the reality of our situation and discovering better how to pray.

J. Oswald Sanders writes in *Spiritual Leadership*,

> The Bible often explains prayer as spiritual warfare (Ephesians 6:12). In this struggle phase of prayer, three personalities are engaged. Between God and the devil stands the Christian at prayer. Though weak alone, the Christian plays a strategic role in the struggle between the dragon and the Lamb. The praying Christian wields no personal power and authority, but authority delegated by the victorious Christ to whom that faithful believer is united by faith. Faith is like a network through which the victory won on Calvary reaches the devil's captives and delivers them from darkness into light (p. 89).

Our world is waiting for praying Christians who understand their place in the plans and purposes of God. Darkness is never dispelled by shouting at it, but by allowing light to shine through it. May the light of Christ shine through you as you take seriously this call to prayer in the midst of warfare. My prayer is that this study would truly be a devotional journey for you. An opportunity to draw near to the Lord Jesus and see Him as Conqueror, Victorious One and King of Kings.

the reality of the war

My favorite Bible story is found in 2 Kings 6.
It is the story of the prophet Elisha and his involvement
in the war between Israel and the Arameans.

SEEING THE UNSEEN

The king of the Arameans had declared war against
Israel. That wasn't a good thing for Israel with its smaller
army. The Aramean king called his generals together and
gave them the battle plans for the attack on Israel. The one
thing that the king hadn't planned on was that God was lis-
tening to the strategy as well. God told Elisha about the
enemy plans. Elisha then immediately passed the information on to the king of Israel. With his much smaller army, the
Israelite king simply moved his army out of the way and
avoided defeat.

After a couple of fiascoes like this, the king of the
Arameans had had it. He called his generals in and demand-
ed who was leaking the information to the Israelites. His generals explained that it wasn't any of them, but the prophet
Elisha who had revealed the plans. They explained to the
king that Elisha knew everything that happened, even the

things in the king's own bedchamber. That thought obviously upset the king!

So he began to make plans to take care of this prophet who was interfering in his attempts at conquest. The king's new strategy was really simple. Go after one man . . . Elisha! In 2 Kings 6, the story continues with Elisha and his young servant in the little village of Dothan. We can imagine what it must have been like that morning. The servant gets up first, as was his custom, to go outside and prepare breakfast for his master. As he walks outside he looks in terror about him, as he sees the entire army of the Arameans surrounding the tiny village. He rushes back in and wakes up the prophet. Can't you see Elisha walking outside the hut, muttering and rubbing the sleep from his eyes? The first words out of his mouth are amazing,

> *"Those who are with us are more than those who are with them."* His young servant had to be thinking, "Wait a minute. There's just two of us. Prophets must be lousy mathematicians."

Then Elisha begins to pray. What is astonishing in his prayer is what he doesn't pray. He doesn't begin to panic in prayer,

> "Oh Lord, save us from this army." Instead, there is this calm, yet amazing request.
>
> "Lord, open this young man's eyes." And if it would be permissible, I would add to my paraphrase what I believe is implied.
>
> "Lord, open this young man's eyes so that he can see what is already there."

His prayer was answered immediately as his servant's eyes were opened and he saw, surrounding the army of the Arameans, the army of heaven. A host of angels, decked out in battle armor, wasready to move at God's command.

I'll let you read the conclusion of the story on your own. It has a *fascinating* finish. The point of the story for our purposes is that Elisha did not ask God to send angels. With his prophet's discernment he saw or sensed their presence. His prayer was for his young servant, that he too, would be able to know of the protective presence of God's angels on their behalf.

REAL REALITY

The Bible teaches, from beginning to end, of the existence of the invisible world, the world of the spirit. A world of angels and demons, yet a world that we touch daily as those who have been given, not merely a body, but also a spirit. This invisible world is a tough sell for many of us today. We tend to focus on that which our senses tell us is real. Things we can touch, taste, smell, hear, or see, are those which seem to be real to us. An invisible world of the spirit seems a bit unreal or mystical.

Because of that, even we who firmly believe that the Bible is God's Word can become practical deists. We can go through life believing Bible stories, but never expect to see the reality of them in our own lives. We can firmly defend the supernatural events of Scripture, but deny that they are impacting us today.

One of the things I love about the way God's Word presents the things of the spirit, is the way it shies away from the mystical or unreal. It presents the unseen world as simply a matter-of-fact. There are things that are seen; there are things that are unseen. Both are real. One is not more real than the other. The invisible world is not a matter of myth but of solid, well-grounded reality.

Jesus had a firm grasp of this reality. He was aware of and interacted with this invisible world on a regular basis. After His baptism, Jesus went into the wilderness for forty days of prayer and fasting. During this time He encountered the devil and faced a time of temptation. This head-to-head battle is not presented with a flourish as if to say, "This is a unique, once-for-all, battle reserved only for the Son of God." Instead, it almost seems as though it is a model of what may happen to *any* of the Lord's followers who makes a decision to follow the direction of God, at all costs. At any rate, the battle in the wilderness is not waged with miraculous signs, but with a clear-headed use of the Word of God to counter the enemy's suggestions.

PUTTING SATAN BEHIND

As Jesus moved through His years of ministry in His earthly body, He encounterd the invisible realm a number of times. There was the time He was preparing to go to Jerusalem and Peter spoke up against it. Jesus turned to him, and we can almost see Him pointing His finger in Peter's direction as He said,

"Get behind me Satan."

How unnerving that must have been for Simon Peter! I don't believe Jesus was calling Peter, "Satan," but rather was responding to Satan himself. Jesus understood how Satan could put words into the mouths of others, like Peter, and simply went to the root of the problem with His rebuke. By the way, if Satan could put his thoughts into the mind of the Apostle Peter, do you suppose he can do the same for us? I'm convinced that one of the major reasons for the many commands given in Scriptures regarding watching what you say, is the possibility that our words unchecked, may contain our enemy's thoughts.

HEALING OF A CRIPPLED WOMAN

There is another encounter with the unseen world that gives great insight into Jesus' beliefs concerning the role of the enemy in human affairs. It concerns the healing of a woman who had experienced a crippling for eighteen years. She was so bent over that she couldn't stand up straight. Jesus healed her on the Sabbath, and in response to His critics said,

> *"Should not this woman, a daughter of Abraham, whom Satan has kept bound for eighteen long years, be set free on the Sabbath day from what bound her?"* (Luke 13:16).

Jesus believed and taught that the enemy can at least cause some illnesses. He did not teach that all illness is from Satan, but that some may find its source in the spirit world.

And have you ever noticed, as you read the Gospels, how many times demons manifested themselves in the midst of Jesus' times of teaching? Jesus gave us a great model for dealing with the demonic. He interrupted His teaching just long enough to get rid of the distraction, then turned immediately back to His teaching. His focus was not on the kingdom of darkness, but on *God's* kingdom. Jesus did not have a deliverance ministry, in the sense that He went out looking for demons to cast out of people. He went about proclaiming the kingdom of heaven. When a demon had the audacity to interrupt, Jesus dealt decisively with it. Then He went right back to proclaiming the advance of the kingdom of God.

PAUL AND THE BATTLE

The Apostle Paul continued the attitude of His Master toward the invisible world. He clearly saw Satan as a real, created being, who was scheming against God and those who followed the ways of God. In 2 Corinthians 2:10-11, Paul spoke of the importance of forgiveness, *"in order that Satan might not outwit us. For we are not unaware of his schemes."* Later in 2 Corinthians he spoke of the god of this age (a clear reference to Satan) who blinds the minds of unbelievers. In 1 Timothy 4:1, Paul warned us that in later times (ours?) some would abandon the faith and follow deceiving spirits and things taught by demons.

It was Paul who began to develop a military terminology for this spiritual conflict. He referred to Christians as soldiers. He told us that we do not wage war as this world does, but rather we use spiritual weapons. Then in Ephesians 6:10-18, he gave us this great treatise on spiritual warfare with special emphasis on putting on the armor of God.

Finally, be strong in the Lord and in his mighty power. Put on the full armor of God so that you can take your stand against the devil's schemes. For our struggle is not against flesh and blood, but against the rulers, against the authorities, against the powers of this dark world and against the spiritual forces of evil in the heavenly realms. Therefore put on the full armor of God, so that when the day of evil comes, you may be able to stand your ground, and after you have done everything, to stand. Stand firm then, with the belt of truth buckled around your waist, with the breastplate of righteousness in place, and with your feet fitted with the readiness that comes from the gospel of peace. In addition to all this, take up the shield of faith, with which you can extinguish all the flaming arrows of the evil one. Take the helmet of salvation and the sword of the Spirit, which is the word of God. And pray in the Spirit on all occasions with all kinds of prayers and requests. With this in mind, be alert and always keep on praying for all the saints.

SERIOUSNESS OF THE BATTLE

Not to be left out, the Apostle Peter added his teaching concerning the battle in 1 Peter 5:8, *"Be self-controlled and alert. Your enemy the devil prowls around like a roaring lion looking for someone to devour."* In his second letter, he wrote of angels who sinned, whom God sent to hell to be held for judgment (2 Peter 2:4). In his short letter, Jude also spoke of these fallen angels, and gave us the amazing story of how the archangel Michael got into a dispute with the devil over the body of Moses (Jude 9).

It's obvious the New Testament authors take spiritual warfare seriously. We ignore it to our detriment and danger. Certainly some may go too far in their practice of this doctrine. We often hear reference to some Christian teachers who see a demon behind every bush. I doubt demons are much interested in bushes, but the point is well taken. If we are not careful, we can end up focusing more on the devil than on Jesus. But much of the church has taken the opposite tact of simply ignoring or denying the devil.

Let me share a pretty scary story of the dangers of ignoring the devil. I grew up in a Bible-believing, conservative church in Indiana. I am so appreciative of the solid foundation of Bible knowledge I received as a child and young man. Yet, in spite of teaching and believing the Bible, Satan was pretty much ignored. His existence was affirmed, but practical warfare teaching was absent. So much so, that in our high school youth group we thought it would be fun to have a séance. Innocently, without awareness of the dangers we were dealing with, we played games that dealt with a reality that had escaped our attention.

For most Christian young people today, participating in a séance would be unthinkable. Over thirty years ago, the myopic teaching on spiritual reality allowed for such a possibility. By the way, the Lord was gracious to us in our innocence and protected us from harm. Even so, years later I personally made sure to renounce any such involvement, however innocent, in an occult activity such as a séance. It is just such an incident that shows the great need for balanced teaching in the area of spiritual warfare.

FINDING BIBLICAL BALANCE

C.S. Lewis gives us great insight into these opposite errors in *The Screwtape Letters*.

There are two equal and opposite errors into which our race can fall about the devils. One is to disbelieve in their existence. The other is to believe, and to feel an excessive and unhealthy interest in them. They themselves are equally pleased by both errors and hail a materialist or a magician with the same delight (Preface, p. ix).

My purpose in this book is to help restore that broad biblical middle ground to the thinking and practice of the church.

The issue here really is: What does the Bible say? It is not a matter of personal experience or perception. Experience and perception can be distorted. It is also not a matter of personal like or dislike. Occasionally I run into people who will say something like this: "Well, it's okay for you to teach on spiritual warfare, but I'm just not into that sort of thing." It really doesn't matter whether you are "into" spiritual warfare or not. The only issue is, "How are you doing in the battle? Are you winning or losing?" We don't get to vote on this. It's not a game where you can take your ball and go home.

God's Word is clear,

> *"For our struggle is not against flesh and blood, but against the rulers, against the authorities, against the powers of this dark world and against the spiritual forces of evil in the heavenly realms"* (Ephesians 6:12).

Spiritual warfare is a reality that must be faced! It won't go away. It is time to prepare ourselves to wage war, not as the world does, but with the weapons provided by the Spirit of God (2 Corinthians 10:3-4).

keeping our spiritual armor ready for warfare

1. Have you ever had problems believing what the Bible says about the spirit world? What has helped you to believe in the reality of such things as the activity of the devil in your own life?

2. Do you believe that Jesus had "special advantages" as He waged war with Satan in the wilderness during His 40 days of fasting? Do you believe that believers today resist temptation in the same way that Jesus did? If you had to resist Satan directly by your use of memorized Scripture, how do you think you would do?

3. Jesus rebuked Peter and called him Satan because of his words. How easy do you think it is for Satan to inspire words in believers today? What are good ways to make sure Satan does not use our mouths?

4. Demons often interrupted the teaching of Jesus. Do you believe that they can do that today in the church? Have you ever experienced what you believed to be demon activity? What did you do about it?

5. What do you believe C.S. Lewis meant when he said that demons "hail a materialist or a magician with the same delight"? Have you ever felt like you went "overboard" in your interest in teaching about the devil?

6. Take time to renounce all occult practices in your life, however innocent (examples: Ouija boards, seances, fortune telling, tarot cards, occult-themed movies, books or games).

chapter 2

the nature of our enemy

> "One of the things that surprised me when I first read the New Testament seriously was that it talked about a Dark Power in the universe—a mighty evil spirit who was held to be the Power behind death and disease, and sin.
>
> . . . .
>
> [Christianity] thinks it is a civil war, a rebellion, and that we are living in a part of the universe occupied by the rebel.
>
> "Enemy-occupied territory—that is what this world is. Christianity is the story of how the rightful king has landed, you might say, landed in disguise, and is calling us all to take place in a great campaign of sabotage. When you go to church you are really listening-in to the secret wireless from our friends: that is why the enemy is so anxious to prevent us from going."
>
> C.S. Lewis—*Mere Christianity*

NOT FLESH AND BLOOD

If the church is at war, then there must be an enemy. Paul begins describing the nature of our enemy in Ephesians 6 by telling us who the enemy is not. Ephesians 6:12 says our struggle is not against flesh and blood. Think about this for a minute. Think about everyone you know on this planet. At least for me, the people I hang around with all have flesh and blood. So Paul tells us this: If you can see them, or touch them—if they have flesh and blood—they are not your enemy! They might be taking the enemy's side. Or even doing the enemy's work. But they are not the enemy.

Instead, Paul described the enemy in dramatic fashion: rulers, authorities, powers of this dark world, spiritual forces of evil in the heavenly realms. We're not allowed by the text to presume that Paul was talking about rulers, authorities or powers of nations here. He just told us that flesh and blood was not the problem. We're contending against *spiritual* beings.

Most biblical scholars view Paul's description as somewhat a hierarchy of hell. There is much discussion trying to define exactly who or what each of these beings is. I have to tell you that I don't care. Really! I don't really care how hell is organized. I'm not interested in knowing too much about the kingdom of darkness. I'd much rather spend my time focusing on the kingdom of *God*.

Many believers get too excited about stories of the demonic. Are there stories of the demonic? You bet! But what does it tell us when we get more excited about demon exorcism than telling the good news of Jesus to someone? Let's learn what we need to know to walk in victory, but keep our focus on the Lord. I do need to add that there are some scholars, and intercessors who go a bit deeper in the study of some of these matters, not for satisfying curiosity, but for ministry purposes.

SATAN'S ORIGIN

It is really impossible to deal with the issue of spiritual warfare without spending at least some time looking at what

God's Word says about Satan. His origin shrouded in the mists of ancient history, Satan is always presented in Scripture as a very real being. Not a myth, nor merely a sense of evil, he is a created being who has set himself up against God and those who serve God. The predominant view of Satan among Christians today is that he was an angel who rebelled against God. In his rebellion, he led a host of angels to move against the purposes of God and who were all eventually expelled from heaven. Nowhere in Scripture is all of this said as clearly as our curiosity would require. But then, God is not required to tell us anything at all about His enemy and ours.

Many would look to the Old Testament passage in Isaiah 14 to give us a glimpse of Satan and his fall from glory. The description of Lucifer and his self-centered rebellion against the Most High certainly fits what we know of Satan. Though the prophet clearly addressed the king of Babylon in this text, it appears that he spoke beyond this real-time prince, to a power behind him.

> *How you have fallen from heaven, O morning star, son of the dawn!*
> *You have been cast down to the earth, you who once laid low the nations!*
> *You said in your heart, "I will ascend to heaven; I will raise my throne above the stars of God; I will sit enthroned on the mount of assembly, on the utmost heights of the sacred mountain. I will ascend above the tops of the clouds; I will make myself like the Most High."*
> *But you are brought down to the grave, to the depths of the pit* (Isaiah 14:12-15).

The Prophet Ezekiel employed a similar strategy as he prophesied concerning the Prince of Tyre. The description given cannot in any literal way actually refer to a human prince. I believe that Ezekiel, as Isaiah before him, was referred to the evil spirit behind the human prince and in so doing, gave us a glimpse into the origin and nature of Satan.

> *You were the model of perfection, full of wisdom and perfect in beauty.*
> *You were in Eden, the garden of God;*
> *Every precious stone adorned you:*
> *Ruby, topaz and emerald, chrysolite, onyx and jasper,*
> *sapphire, turquoise and beryl.*
> *Your settings and mountings were made of gold;*
> *On the day you were created they were prepared.*
> *You were anointed as a guardian cherub,*
> *For so I ordained you.*
> *You were on the holy mount of God;*
> *you walked among the fiery stones.*
> *You were blameless in your ways from the day you were created till wickedness was found in you.*
> *Through your widespread trade you were filled with violence,*
> *and you sinned.*
> *So I drove you in disgrace from the mount of God,*
> *and I expelled you, O guardian cherub, from among the fiery stones.*
> *Your heart became proud on account of your beauty,*

*and you corrupted your wisdom because of
your splendor.
So I threw you to the earth;
I made a spectacle of you before kings*
(Ezekiel 28:12-17).

It is not only the Old Testament that hints at the origins of
Satan. The Book of Revelation with its theme of cosmic conflict quite naturally also deals much with the enemy.
Revelation chapter 12 gives us a glimpse into heaven and the
conflict there that has spilled over onto our planet. The
imagery of Satan here is that of a great red dragon. This dragon fomented rebellion in heaven itself and war broke out.

*And there was war in heaven. Michael and his
angels fought against the dragon, and the dragon
and his angels fought back. But he was not strong
enough, and they lost their place in heaven. The
great dragon was hurled down—that ancient serpent
called the devil, or Satan, who leads the whole world
astray. He was hurled to the earth, and his angels
with him* (Revelation 12:7-9).

It would be conjecture to ask questions here. The Bible
doesn't tell us why Satan rebelled. It doesn't describe for us
what angelic warfare is like. It doesn't tell us how many
angels followed Satan, though many would point to
Revelation 12:4, "*His tail swept a third of the stars out of the
sky and flung them to the earth,*" as an indication that perhaps a third of the angelic host followed Satan's leadership.
Most of us believe that those fallen angels are later described

in Scripture as demons. But understand that the Bible does not clearly say that. I do believe that this is the simplest explanation of the origin of the demonic host.

Revelation 12 gives us a graphic picture of the impact of this heavenly war on our planet:

Now have come the salvation and the power and the kingdom of our God,
and the authority of his Christ.
For the accuser of our brothers,
Who accuses them before our God day and night has been hurled down.
They overcame him by the blood of the Lamb and by the word of their testimony;
they did not love their lives so much as to shrink from death.
Therefore rejoice, you heavens and you who dwell in them!
But woe to the earth and the sea, because the devil has gone down to you!
He is filled with fury,
because he knows that his time is short
(Revelation 12:10-12).

SATAN'S NAMES

Regardless of our uncertainty concerning the origins of Satan and the spirits under his control, Scripture is definitely not silent regarding him. He is a being of many names: Lucifer, Satan, the devil, the dragon, the father of lies, a thief, a murderer. It could be said that he is so evil, that one name will not suffice for him. In contrast, Jesus is so good, that it takes many names in Scripture to even begin to describe His attributes.

The following Scriptures give names to our enemy that help us understand more of his purposes:

1. Satan—Job 1:6; Zechariah 3:2; Mark 4:15; 2 Corinthians 11:14; 12:7; Revelation 12:9; 20:2,7.
2. Accuser—Revelation 12:10
3. Morning star ("Lucifer" in Latin Vulgate)—Isaiah 14:12
4. Dragon—Revelation 12:7,9; 20:2
5. Devil (33 times in 32 verses)—e.g., Revelation 12:9; 1 Peter 5:8
6. Ancient serpent—Revelation 12:9
7. Murderer—John 8:44
8. Liar—John 8:44
9. Deceiver—Revelation 20:8,10
10. Prince of this world—John 12:31; 16:11
11. Ruler of the kingdom of the air—Ephesians 2:2
12. Tempter—Matthew 4:3; 1 Thessalonians 3:5
13. Evil one—Matthew 5:37; 13:38; Ephesians 6:16
14. God of this age—2 Corinthians 4:4

SATAN'S ANTICS

Mark Bubeck has written a powerful book entitled, *The Adversary*. In this book he organized a Bible study around the topics of Satan's power, strategy and destiny. I've put the following material under those same topics and drawn from Mark's excellent work.

1. Satan's power
   a. Not even a Christian can ignore Satan's power to defeat him apart from God's provided victory. God's armor must be used (Ephesians 6:11-12).

b. He is absolute sovereign over the realm of demons. Scripture is clear that he has a kingdom (Luke11:14-18; Matthew 12:26). The Bible speaks of demons or evil spirits. These are the ground troops of Satan. As a created being, Satan cannot be everywhere at once as God can. He must work through other spirits. The Bible does teach of hierarchies of evil spirits . . . some, such as principalities and powers, rule nations and influence cultures.

c. He has the power to oppose the mightiest of angels (Jude 9; Daniel 10:12-13).

d. He maneuvers and holds in bondage the realm of lost men. "We know that we are the children of God, and that the whole world is under the control of the evil one" (1 John 5:19).

e. Satan's power is limited by the will of God (Job 1:10-12).

2. *Satan's strategy*

a. He authored sin and continues to agitate man to sin (Genesis 3:1-6).

b. He causes sickness and suffering (Acts 10:38).

c. He has the power of death (Hebrews 2:14).

d. He injects wicked purposes into men's hearts (John 13:2).

e. He can personally enter and control a man (John 13:27).

f. He provides snares or traps for men (1 Timothy 3:7).

g. He seeks to take away the Word of God from our understanding (Mark 4:15).

h. He attempts to torment God's servants (Luke 22:31).

i. He can hinder God's servants from carrying out their

desires (1 Thessalonians 2:18).

j.   He casts God's servants into prison (Revelation 2:10).

k.   He accuses believers before God (Revelation 12:10).

3. *Satan's Destiny*

a.   He is under the sentence of doom (Isaiah 14:15).

b.   He is under an unending curse (Genesis 3:14-15).

c.   He will be cast out of heaven (if not already—Revelation 12:7-10).

d.   He will be bound in the bottomless pit (Revelation 20:1-3).

e.   He will be consigned eternally to the lake of fire (Revelation 20:10).

A Bible study about Satan may not seem profitable. It certainly is not enjoyable (at least it wasn't to me). Its value lies in understanding that spiritual warfare is not about dualism. The Bible does not present the view of two equal and opposing forces fighting it out for control of the universe. It is not merely good versus evil. Scripture clearly shows one almighty, all-powerful God, Creator of all things. Satan, as powerful as he is, is simply a creature gone wrong. The outcome of the war has never been in doubt. What is critical now are the choices you and I make each day as combatants in this great cosmic battle.

1. How do you feel about the statement, "if they have flesh and blood, they aren't your enemy"? How do we handle people who seem to be doing the work of the enemy?

2. Do you believe that Satan is a fallen angel? Why or why not? Do you agree with the author that demons are probably fallen angels?

3. How would you answer those who believe that Satan is merely a personification of evil?

4. Scripture assigns many names to Satan. Is there one more than another that stands out in your experience of the enemy? Why?

5. Have you ever gone through a Bible study on Satan before? Has your church dealt with this topic? Why do you suppose churches often ignore this study?

chapter 3

everyday combat readiness

I returned from a Christian conference so excited about prayer that I determined I would get up early the next morning and spend a significant amount of time in prayer. I set my alarm clock for 5:30 a.m. (Yes, God is up then!) I got up and prepared myself for prayer. I had no sooner begun praying when suddenly, I had this overpowering urge . . . to wash my car! My mind began to be filled with images of my dirty car and the hectic schedule for the day ahead that wouldn't allow me to get it washed. It became so overwhelming that I found myself getting off my knees and getting ready to go wash my car. Then there came flooding into my mind a question, "Dave, when was the last time you had an overwhelming desire to wash your car at 5:30 in the morning?" The answer of course was, "Never!" So then, where did the thought originate to quit praying and go wash my car? I began that morning to realize that the devil wanted me to wash my car, God wanted me to pray, and I wanted to pray. It made the decision to stay and pray very simple. Awareness of the enemy's attack was a key to victory in my prayer time that day.

BE ALERT!

Paul wrotes, *"Be alert, and always keep on praying. . . ."* (Ephesians 6:18). Alertness is a critical area for victory in spiritual warfare that is often ignored by Christians to their grave danger. The commands of Scripture are many: be alert, watch, be careful, be on your guard. The authors of Scripture believed we were in some sort of danger that required an awareness and alertness on our part. Yet so many of us wander through this life totally unaware of the dangers that lurk on every side.

I believe 90% of the battle in the area of spiritual warfare is simply being aware that there is indeed a battle going on around and in us. Look at this from the perspective of actual physical warfare. Can you imagine a group of soldiers in the midst of a battle forgetting where they are? Imagine . . . planes flying over head, cannon firing, bullets whizzing by . . . and they decide to go on a picnic. Forgetting completely about the battle raging around them, they pack a nice lunch and take off across the landscape looking for a nice spot to sit and eat. As they walk, every now and then one of them gets injured; occasionally, one is killed, and they stop and ask the question, "How can such bad things happen to such good people?" Recognize the question? What's your response to such a group of soldiers? Would you think they are warriors with mental problems . . . failing to comprehend reality? Right! And so are we when we wander through our days with no awareness of the reality of the spiritual battles we face each day.

PUT ON THE ARMOR!

What can help remind us daily of the reality of this warfare? The Ephesians 6 passage gives us a wonderful gift to help us walk in awareness. It is called the armor of God. I grew up in the church and consequently heard about the armor of God many times. I heard it taught, analyzed and dissected. As I look back, it seems like we did everything except what the Bible told us to do. Put it on! That's right, the Bible simply commands us to put on the armor.

Many years ago, when I finally understood what to do with it, I began putting on the armor of God every morning. I've trained myself to put on the armor daily as I begin my shower. The water hits me and it serves as a reminder to begin to pray and put on my spiritual protection for the day. It's okay to do that in the shower . . . it's rustproof armor.

Some would simply say, "Well, I'm a Christian so I already have my armor and I don't need this exercise of putting it on daily." Good for you! As for me, I need the daily reminder. Ephesians was written to Christians, but Paul told them to do something regarding the armor. Put it on! How? Remember the old hymn, "Stand Up, Stand Up for Jesus"? The third verse says, "Put on the gospel armor, each piece put on with prayer." Maybe it's time to quit just singing it and begin to put on the armor in prayer each day.

When I put on God's armor daily I am reminded that I am in a battle. Awareness floods into my soul that I have awakened to danger that day. But even more there is the quiet assurance that I follow the Commander-in-Chief of the Lord's Armies. He has provided both victory and protection for me in the midst of the day's struggles. He has loaned me His very own armor. So with great joy, I pray, gratefully accepting and clothing myself with His armor. Alert to the battle, prepared through prayer, I move through the day's battles, not with fear, but with confidence in my Lord's victory.

There is another aspect to the armor that is tremendously exciting. Do you realize that every part of the armor corresponds to an attribute of Jesus? When we put on the helmet of salvation, we realize that Jesus' very name means God is my salvation. The breastplate of righteousness reminds us that Jesus has become our righteousness. The fact that Jesus is the truth is brought home as we put on the belt of truth.

The Prince of Peace Himself reminds us to fasten to our feet the readiness of the gospel of peace. As we take up the shield of faith, we remember the Scripture references that speak of Him as the shield that goes before us (e.g., Deuteronomy 33:29). Wielding the sword of the Lord, God's Word becomes a natural, daily activity for those who follow the Living Word of God. Putting on the armor is becoming clothed with Christ!

GET READY!

In addition to being clothed with the armor of God, James gives us some wonderful steps for combat readiness in James 4:7-8, *"Submit yourselves, then, to God. Resist the devil, and he will flee from you. Come near to God and he will come near to you. Wash your hands, you sinners, and purify your hearts, you double-minded."*

This is boot camp for believers. Basic training for those preparing for battle. And if you're not preparing for battle, you are preparing for defeat. Spiritual preparation begins when we:

1. *Submit to God.* There is no outright rebellion against God in our lives that would give the devil a foothold.
2. *Come near to God.* This is a prayer life focused on intimacy with the Lord. This life of intimacy is a place of

protection in the midst of warfare.

3. *Wash our hands and purify our hearts.* This call to holiness is essential if we are to stand victorious.

In the midst of submitting to God, drawing near to Him, and walking in holiness, we are able to *resist the devil.*

PRAY!

It is important to understand that we do not simply do these things once and then leave them behind. Warfare is constant. We are called to vigilance. Submission, intimacy, holiness and resistance to the devil will need to be a part of every day's prayer life. Let me suggest some further steps for practical preparation for everyday warfare that need to be a part of your daily prayers:

1. *Prayer of protection.* I believe it is appropriate to ask the Lord for protection each day for ourselves, our family, and others for whom we may have responsibility. This involves both spiritual and physical protection. It is dangerous to assume we are protected. I believe the Lord would have us ask in dependence upon Him. Scriptures that teach us how God is concerned with our protection can be found in Ezra 8:21-23; Job 1:10; Psalm 91, and Jesus' prayer for the disciples in John 17:12 and 15.

2. *Prayer for discernment.* In the midst of daily life it is vital that we understand what is of the enemy and what may simply be the circumstances of life. When Paul wrote that *"we are not unaware of Satan's schemes,"* he implied an ability to discern the hand of the enemy in the midst of life's happenings. This is especially vital for a local church

as they deal with individuals and circumstances that may be creating problems. "Lord, is this the hand of our enemy at work?" may be a most appropriate prayer.

3. *Prayer for opened spiritual eyes.* Paul wrote in 2 Corinthians 4:4 that the god of this age has blinded the minds of unbelievers. One of our most important prayers should be for God to remove the blindfolds from the minds of those whom we may have the opportunity to reach with the gospel of Jesus Christ.

4. *Prayer of blessing.* A wonderful privilege has been granted to us to pray God's blessing upon those in need. Whether it is prayer for those in your own family, or prayer for those on the other side of the planet, the prayer of blessing allows the light to attack the darkness. It is a word of hope in the midst of despair.

5. *Prayer for spiritual leaders.* There is an all-out attack by the forces of hell against spiritual leaders. We need to be praying for our pastors every day as well as other leaders in our churches.

6. *Prayer for revival.* There is nothing that Satan hates like revival. An awakened church is his worst fear. As we pray daily for a great awakening of the body of Christ, we are doing great damage to the kingdom of darkness. One of the great moves of God's Spirit today is in calling the church to fervent prayer for revival.

7. *Prayer for completion of the task of world evangelism.* The advance of God's kingdom throughout the world continues as people from every tribe, tongue and nation give their lives to Jesus. Our prayers must reflect and reinforce this great move of God against the forces of darkness.

1. Do you have any consistent way to keep yourself aware of the reality of spiritual warfare? If so, share that with others in your study group. Why do you suppose it is so easy to forget that we are at war?

2. Have you been taught before about putting on the armor of God on a daily basis? Does this seem too simplistic to you? Can we use an analogy like that of the armor and make it a part of our daily prayer life?

3. What does the Scripture that we are to be clothed with Christ mean to you? Does putting on the armor help you experience that in a more real way?

4. Do you believe that young and new Christians are taught enough about basic training for spiritual warfare? How can your church better prepare your members for warfare?

5. How does prayer for revival become a part of our warfare? Is prayer for revival a part of your daily prayer life? How can a church or small group within a church train its members in revival praying?

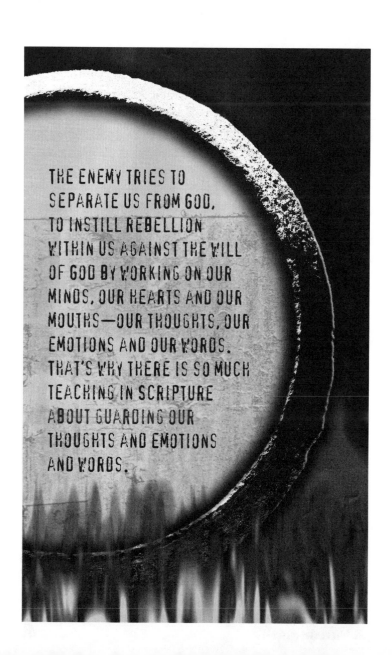

THE ENEMY TRIES TO SEPARATE US FROM GOD, TO INSTILL REBELLION WITHIN US AGAINST THE WILL OF GOD BY WORKING ON OUR MINDS, OUR HEARTS AND OUR MOUTHS—OUR THOUGHTS, OUR EMOTIONS AND OUR WORDS. THAT'S WHY THERE IS SO MUCH TEACHING IN SCRIPTURE ABOUT GUARDING OUR THOUGHTS AND EMOTIONS AND WORDS.

three areas of conflict

One of my favorite teachers in the area of spiritual warfare is Dean Sherman of Youth With a Mission (YWAM). Twenty years ago I heard him teach that the three major areas of spiritual warfare are all internal. They are the mind, the heart and the mouth. That's very different from what many others would teach. Christians often want to focus on the spectacular—stories of demons and exorcisms. It's not that those spectacular stories are not true. It's just that most spiritual warfare is of a little more mundane nature. Mundane, but still deadly.

The enemy tries to separate us from God, to instill rebellion within us against the will of God by working on our minds, our hearts and our mouths—our thoughts, our emotions and our words. That's why there is so much teaching in Scripture about guarding our thoughts and emotions and words.

> *"The mind of sinful man is death, but the mind controlled by the Spirit is life and peace. . . ."* (Romans 8:6).

"Above all else, guard your heart, for it is the wellspring of life" (Proverbs 4:23).

"For out of the overflow of the heart the mouth speaks. The good man brings good things out of the good stored up in him, and the evil man brings evil things out of the evil stored up in him. But I tell you that men will have to give account on the day of judgment for every careless word they have spoken. For by your words you will be acquitted, and by your words you will be condemned" (Matthew 12:34b-37).

These are but a few of hundreds of Scriptures that refer to the mind, heart and mouth. Spiritual warfare rages in these areas.

THE MIND

You wake up in the morning and the thoughts from yesterday's events bring worry or stress. You think about the day ahead of you and fear or tension fills your heart. Your concern over family members or other relationships begins to weigh down your day before it ever really gets going. Many of us look at such situations as just normal life. But there is a warfare aspect to these thoughts. God's Word teaches us that He wants us to lay aside fear . . . that worry and anxiety are to be given over to Him. He wants to set us free from these thoughts that damage our lives.

If God wants us free from such thoughts, you can count on the fact that the devil wants us to wallow in these fears. The Christian that spends his or her time worrying or in fear is a Christian who is being made ineffective in kingdom matters. When the enemy can manipulate our thoughts away from trusting God, he has won a victory.

One great area of concern for Christians needs to be the things we allow into our minds. Our thoughts quite naturally will focus on whatever ideas or images we have taken into our lives. In the age of mass media, that makes the devil's work much easier. All he has to do is influence a (relatively) few television or movie producers, some newspaper editors, authors, and throw in a few popular musicians and most of his work in distorting our thoughts is done. That's why it is so important that we carefully monitor what we allow into our minds.

I'm not suggesting that it would be good, or even possible to never see anything produced that is contrary to Christian thought. What I am saying *strongly* is that we must learn to evaluate what we watch on television, or read, or listen to, in the light of the truth of God's Word. As Christians, we must learn to critically analyze the thoughts and ideas that are thrown at us daily and begin to screen out the lies of the enemy.

Part of our difficulty comes from lazy thinking. We have become so accustomed to being spoon-fed mentally that it requires great effort to rouse ourselves from just accepting what we hear to the point of discerning the intent behind words and images. This is not just pointing to the youngest among us. Every generation living today has been affected by this laziness of thought. Have you ever read something by an author from two hundred years ago? It can be so difficult to follow. He often follows a line of logic through to its natural conclusion, and that can be so confusing to the modern mind. It's an example of how we have slipped into a mode of not critically analyzing what we read, watch or listen to. Could this be why Paul commands us to take every thought captive? Warfare rages in the mind.

C.S. Lewis, in *The Screwtape Letters*, has the senior devil, Screwtape, offer this diabolical advice to his young nephew, who is a tempter:

> It sounds as if you supposed that argument was the way to keep him out of the Enemy's [Jesus'] clutches. That might have been so if he had lived a few centuries earlier. At that time the humans still knew pretty well when a thing was proved and when it was not; and if it was proved they really believed it. They still connected thinking with doing and were prepared to alter their way of life as the result of a chain of reasoning. But what with the weekly press and other such weapons we have largely altered that (p. 1).

Derek Prince writes, "The battleground on which this war is being fought is in the minds of humanity. Satan has built up strongholds of prejudice and unbelief in the minds of the human race to keep them from receiving the truth of the gospel" (*Spiritual Warfare,* Whitaker House 1987, p. 49).

THE HEART

The heart is the second active front for spiritual warfare. The Greek word for heart, *kardia*, encompasses much more than the physical organ that pumps blood through the body. In the Bible, it sometimes refers to the whole person, as in Acts 14:17, *"he . . . fills your hearts with joy."* Heart also focuses on the thought life, the emotions, and even the spiritual life. In regard to spiritual warfare, I want to focus on the heart as the seat of human emotions, and as such, a prime target for the enemy's attacks.

Dr. Wayne Detzler writes of the emotional aspect of the heart as seen in Scripture:

> The heart is joyful when something good happens to us (Acts 2:26; 14:17). By contrast when things go wrong one's heart is consumed with sorrow (John 14:1; Rom. 9:2). Love too is felt in the heart (Matt. 22:37; 2 Cor. 7:3; Phil. 1:7). When anguish comes upon us, it also descends on the heart (2 Cor. 2:4).

In our day, the emotional aspect of the heart takes a real beating in spiritual warfare. We live in a day when feelings and emotions rule. We have a tendency to be a people who believe that if something feels good, it's okay. By contrast, if it feels bad, then we probably ought to avoid it. In this current atmosphere, it is rather easy for the enemy to manipulate our emotions, and consequently move us into an area of disobedience to God.

Peter's description of the devil as a roaring lion (1 Peter 5:8) speaks powerfully to the ability of our enemy to affect emotions. A lion creeps up quietly on its victims, getting as near as possible before it pounces. Right before it leaps, it emits a horrifying roar that has the effect of paralyzing the prey for just enough time to allow the lion to nab its meal successfully. The roar of the lion has a powerful, paralyzing effect upon our hearts. Satan has discovered this to our detriment. How many times have we been defeated by the lion's roar in our lives?

Satan's roars sometimes come across as whispers in our minds, causing us to doubt those closest to us. It may create fear of failure or rejection. The list is endless of how our enemy plays with our hearts and stirs emotions that lead us away from God's peace and perfect will for our lives.

Christian Psychologist James Dobson authored the book, *Emotions: Can You Trust Them?* Dobson often says he wrote a whole book really just to say one word, "no." You can't trust your emotions. It seems that the key to victory in the area of our emotions is not to deny the reality or power of our emotions, but to submit our emotions to the leadership of our minds. Most of the things we have done that we have wished we could somehow undo happened when we followed our emotions rather than our minds. When the Bible speaks of guarding our hearts, I believe we should allow our minds to provide that protection for our hearts.

THE MOUTH

The third area of spiritual warfare that we face on a daily basis occurs with regard to our mouths. Dean Sherman said, "You can't defeat the devil and let him use your mouth." All too often Christians let the devil do just that.

It's so easy to do. We open our mouths and the first thing out is often the thing we wish we had never said. Words come out so easily . . . words that hurt and damage . . . words that have poison in them. Words may initially sound Christian as we ask for prayer for someone and then continue into gossip or accusation.

God's Word warns of the mouth's dangers:

"The tongue has the power of life and death, and those who love it will eat its fruit" (Proverbs 18:21).

"Set a guard over my mouth, O LORD, keep watch over the door of my lips" (Psalm 141:3).

". . . but no man can tame the tongue. It is a rest-less evil, full of deadly poison. With the tongue we praise our Lord and Father, and with it we curse men, who have been made in God's likeness. Out of the same mouth come praise and cursing. My brothers, this should not be" (James 3:8-10).

Do you recall the story we looked at in the first chapter in which Peter found himself opposing the will of God? Here's the way Mark recounts the event:

He then began to teach them that the Son of Man must suffer many things and be rejected by the eld-ers, chief priests and teachers of the law, and that he must be killed and after three days rise again. He spoke plainly about this, and Peter took him aside and began to rebuke him. But when Jesus turned and looked at his disciples, he rebuked Peter. "Get behind me, Satan!" he said. "You do not have in mind the things of God, but the things of men (Mark 8:31-33).

The words of Peter revealed their source. Satan had whis-pered his lies and deceit into Peter's ears and without dis-cerning this, Peter simply spoke out what seemed like his own thoughts and fears. Jesus discerned the source and addressed Satan as the perpetrator of this attempt to persuade Jesus to avoid the plan of God for His life. Like Peter, we too can be used by the enemy to lead people away unwittingly from God's plan for their lives.

The only way I know to avoid this is to speak less. We so often feel that we must speak up and let our opinions be known. Without careful discernment though, our words can often run counter to the will of God. As one who is mostly verbal, it has been a real struggle to be quieter. It has often been a test of faith. Can I trust God to step into a situation and correct it without my words? Am I the one He calls into every conversation? Though difficult, it has been a source of joy and an area of growth in my life to "bite my tongue" and not offer my opinion on every issue.

Certainly there are times when the opposite response is called for. There comes that time when the Spirit of God requires you to speak up in order to bring the Lord's perspective into a situation. The principle though is the same. We speak (or do not speak) in accordance with the Lord's will. That requires a disciplined tongue. God's Word warns us of idle chatter. It is so often in these unguarded moments that the enemy finds our mouths willing instruments in his war of words.

> Jesus said, *"But I tell you that men will have to give account on the day of judgment for every careless word they have spoken"* (Matthew 12:36).

1. Can you think of areas other than the mind, the heart, and the mouth that are arenas of spiritual warfare? What are they?

2. How should Christians monitor the things they allow into their minds? Is such careful self-evaluation even possible or profitable? Why or why not?

3. Do you agree with the author's contention that we are victims of "lazy thinking"? Why or why not?

4. What would it take in your own life to shift your thinking processes into higher gear?

5. Can you think of a time in which your emotions got you in trouble? Have you ever been aware of your emotions as a battleground for spiritual warfare? Suggest some ways to bring emotions under the control of the mind.

6. What is the most recent time that your words got you in trouble? How have you been able to control what you say?

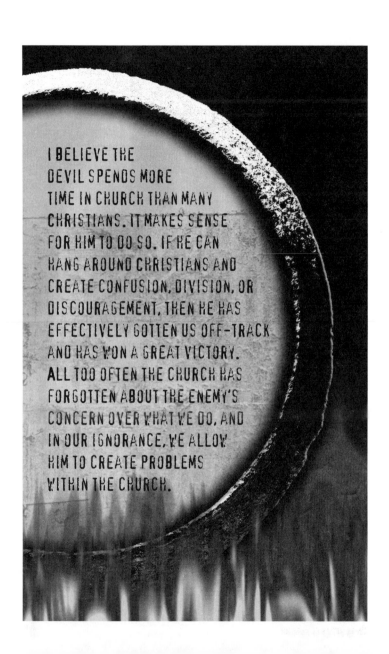

I BELIEVE THE DEVIL SPENDS MORE TIME IN CHURCH THAN MANY CHRISTIANS. IT MAKES SENSE FOR HIM TO DO SO. IF HE CAN HANG AROUND CHRISTIANS AND CREATE CONFUSION, DIVISION, OR DISCOURAGEMENT, THEN HE HAS EFFECTIVELY GOTTEN US OFF-TRACK AND HAS WON A GREAT VICTORY. ALL TOO OFTEN THE CHURCH HAS FORGOTTEN ABOUT THE ENEMY'S CONCERN OVER WHAT WE DO, AND IN OUR IGNORANCE, WE ALLOW HIM TO CREATE PROBLEMS WITHIN THE CHURCH.

the devil goes to church

Have you ever experienced the Sunday Morning Wars?
It happens to Christian families all over the world as they prepare to worship in their local congregations. Why is Sunday morning the one day that it seems everything goes wrong? Kids cry, cars don't work, and parents are unusually on edge with one another. And it doesn't end when we reach the friendly confines of the church building. In some ways, it can intensify.

I've often wondered if the devil pinches babies at just that critical time in the worship service when everyone's attention is focused on the Lord. Or consider the use of technology in our worship services which can be wonderful . . . or can be another opportunity for the devil to distract us as we wait for missed cues, burnt-out lights, PowerPoint operators that keep taking us to the wrong verse of a song, and you can fill in the blank. . . .

I believe the devil spends more time in church than many Christians. It makes sense for him to do so. If he can hang around Christians and create confusion, division, or discouragement, then he has effectively gotten us off-track and has won a great victory. All too often the church has forgotten about the enemy's concern over what we do, and in our ignorance, we allow him to create problems within the church.

CHOOSING SIDES

Jesus certainly expressed His concern over the devil coming to church. In His great high-priestly prayer He prayed, *"My prayer is not that you take them out of the world but that you protect them from the evil one"* (John 17:15). Jesus had experienced the opposition of the enemy and knew that His followers would as well. His prayer for protection should cause us to join with Him in this type of prayer.

There is a very real reason the devil goes to church. The biblical worldview is of a great cosmic battle between the forces of God and the forces of Satan. Christians are those who have changed sides in the battle. Paul writes about this changing of sides in Ephesians 2:2-5:

> . . . in which you used to live when you followed the ways of this world and of the ruler of the kingdom of the air, the spirit who is now at work in those who are disobedient. All of us also lived among them at one time, gratifying the cravings of our sinful nature and following its desires and thoughts. Like the rest, we were by nature objects of wrath. But because of his great love for us, God, who is rich in mercy, made us alive with Christ even when we were dead in transgressions—it is by grace you have been saved.

The enemy of our God has become our enemy. We are not in a neutral position. When Christians gather as the church, we become a real threat to Satan. We are there to worship, to pray, to teach, to instruct and to encourage one another to live and proclaim the kingdom of God and, as such, proclaim the enemy's defeat. It is apparent that he will do all he can to prevent that from happening.

Once again, C.S. Lewis helps us understand this from Satan's perspective in *The Screwtape Letters:*

> One of our great allies at present is the Church itself. Do not misunderstand me. I do not mean the Church as we see her spread out through all time and space and rooted in eternity, terrible as an army with banners. That, I confess, is a spectacle which makes our boldest tempters uneasy. But fortunately, it is quite invisible to these humans (p. 5).

The real danger for us is our being unaware of the enemy's schemes. We approach every difficulty in church as though it's just a natural thing. When churches divide over whether or not to use hymns or contemporary choruses, it is not natural. When the flock turns on the shepherd, it is not natural. When the saints, called to live in love, spend their time criticizing and accusing one another, it is not natural. The devil has come to church!

There is one obvious thing about Satan's attacks . . . he is consistent. He does basically the same things over and over again in church after church, as he has done down through the ages. We might categorize them in these memorable ways: Doubt, Deception, Discouragement and Division.

DOUBT

Sowing doubt has been one of the enemy's weapons from the very beginning. In Eden, the serpent stirred up doubt in Eve, causing her to sin. He caused her (and Adam) to doubt God's word . . . asking the insidious question, *"Has God said . . . ?"* You can almost hear the oily voice continuing, "You don't really believe that do you?" The same voice . . . really! . . . the very same voice is asking the same question today, causing Christians to begin to doubt God and His Word.

Doubt was the weapon Satan used against Jesus in the wilderness. Every temptation was preceded by the word, "if". "*IF* you are the Son of God" the enemy whispers, attempting to instill doubt into Jesus. He still uses the same attack on us.

Doubt can come in many forms. Sometimes it is the frontal attack on the veracity of the Bible. There are many, yes, in the church, who simply do not believe that all of the Bible is truly God's inspired Word. But sometimes the most vicious attack comes on those who do believe in the Bible, but are then led into doubt as to the power of God's Word. "Will that really work?" people ask. Whole segments of Scripture are robbed of their power as Christians relegate them to some other day or time, and fail to appropriate them for themselves. Be careful when trying to explain away a clear meaning of Scripture. It may be that the enemy is raising doubts.

Doubt is also raised as to the nature of God. When tragedies come in life (and they do), even Christians find themselves doubting the love or mercy of God. "How could a loving God cause (or allow) such a thing to happen?" The whispering enemy is again at work to cause God's people to doubt the goodness or power of their God. We're sometimes told that to doubt is natural. Not for those who have tasted of the goodness, mercy and power of God! *Faith* is the natural response to God. Look at Job and the almost inconceivable tragedy that changed his life. Though facing great loss and with tremendous grief, still he spoke words one of the great faith responses in Scripture:

> *"The LORD gave and the LORD has taken away;*
> *may the name of the LORD be praised"* (Job 1:21).

Doubt also comes to the individual believer regarding his or her position in Christ. The enemy continually works at trying to separate us from Christ. He doesn't have the power to do that actually, but he tries to get us to doubt our identity in Christ. The best way to counter that is with the truth of God's Word. Christian author, Neil Anderson, has written much on this topic and has prepared a wonderful list of Scriptures that affirm who we are in Christ.

John 1:12—I am God's child

John 15:15—I am Christ's friend

Romans 5:1—I have been justified

1 Corinthians 6:17—I am united with the Lord and one with Him in spirit

1 Corinthians 6:20—I have been bought with a price; I belong to God

1 Corinthians 12:27—I am a member of Christ's Body

Ephesians 1:1—I am a saint

Ephesians 1:5—I have been adopted as God's child

Ephesians 2:18—I have direct access to God through the Holy Spirit

Colossians 1:14—I have been redeemed and forgiven of all my sins

Colossians 2:10—I am complete in Christ *(The Bondage Breaker)*

DECEPTION

The second weapon that Satan uses against the church is deceit. This shouldn't surprise us since Jesus Himself described Satan as a liar. Satan delights in twisting the truth, confusing people and leading them into error. That's rather obvious when you look at the condition of Christian doctrine, both within and without the church. It may be as subtle as the lack of understanding concerning Christian grace or as obvious as those who deny the inspiration of the Bible.

The Apostle Paul spoke of difficult times for the church in the last days, especially in regard to truth. We are warned of those who are

> *". . . always learning but never able to acknowledge the truth. Just as Jannes and Jambres opposed Moses, so also these men oppose the truth—men of depraved minds, who, as far as the faith is concerned, are rejected"* (2 Timothy 3:7-8).

This passage is so clearly being lived out in the church today that we should easily see the enemy's handiwork. There is no shortage of Bible studies in our churches. But we debate the meaning rather than living out the intent of God's Word. We have fallen into the trap that James warned us about:

> *"Do not merely listen to the word, and so deceive yourselves. Do what it says"* (James 1:22).

*Studying Scripture without **doing** it is one of Satan's great deceits.*

This deception concerning the Word of God leaves the church powerless and unable to function as God has intended. George Otis Jr. delivers a scathing indictment of this powerlessness:

> If ever there was a moment for the Church to stand up and be counted, that moment is now. Unfortunately, American Christendom is in the midst of a debilitating spiritual funk. At almost every turn, supernatural power and insight have given way to religious inertia. Fellowships are growing numerically, but members are not maturing in character. There are programs aplenty, but little fear of God. Most ominously, modern believers seem oblivious to their own unhealthy condition. Having succumbed to the Laodicean Syndrome (see Revelation 3:14-17), they view their compromised state as normal—even blessed.
>
> A troubling, if predictable, consequence of this spiritual self-deception is that the Church has found itself unable to speak into the current crisis with any clarity or consistency. Burdened political leaders seeking direction from Christian clergy and prayer networks report receiving advice that "wanders all over the map". Needing perspicacious wise men, these national decision makers are finding instead blind guides and flesh-clouded counsel. (George Otis Jr., "Fading Light," January 2003).

DISCOURAGEMENT

Hebrews 10:25 is one of the main Scriptures we often use to hit people over the head to attend church:

> *"Let us not give up meeting together, as some are in the habit of doing, but let us encourage one another—and all the more as you see the Day approaching."*

The focus of the passage, however, is not merely attending a meeting, but on the process of encouraging one another.

One of the very practical reasons for this scriptural command is to counter the enemy's strategy of discouraging the believers. Many a faithful Christian who has withstood the more frontal attacks of Satan in the area of morality, truth and righteous living, has found himself blind-sided by discouragement. A few words of criticism here and there, a "down" day, a little loss of fresh vision, a program that didn't go according to plan . . . and suddenly we find ourselves discouraged and wondering if we can go on.

Many great women and men of God have had severe bouts with discouragement and depression. Perhaps the clearest example is that of Elijah following his great victory over the prophets of Baal. In the wake of that victory, Queen Jezebel ordered his execution. In fear, Elijah ran and ended up in this situation in 1 Kings 19:4b:

> He came to a broom tree, sat down under it and prayed that he might die. *"I have had enough, LORD,"* he said. *"Take my life; I am no better than my ancestors.*

Now that is serious discouragement from a great man of God. It took the intervention of the Lord Himself to bring Elijah out of that depressed mood.

You may not have sat under a tree with a desire to die, but discouragement can hit us all. The great word of God to the church in this case is that we are called to be an encouragement to one another. We are to build one another up in our faith. Our gatherings need to be times of great encouragement. The church that is a place of support and edification is a place where the enemy's plans have been thwarted.

There is an old story about discouragement called, "The Devil's Tool Sale."

It was advertised that the Devil was putting his tools up for sale. On that date the tools were laid out for public inspection. They had prices on them, and there were a lot of treacherous instruments: hatred, envy, jealousy, deceit, pride, lying, and so on. Laid apart from the rest of the Devil's tools was a harmless-looking tool, worn more than any of the others and priced very high.

"What's the name of this tool?" asked one of the customers.

"That," the Devil replied, "is discouragement."

"Why have your priced it so high?"

"Because discouragement is more useful to me than all the others. I can pry open and get inside a man's heart with that when I cannot get near him with any other tools. It's badly worn because I use it on almost everyone, since so few people know it belongs to me."

When we begin to understand that discouragement is of the enemy, we can begin to counter it using the weapons of our warfare in Ephesians 6:10-18. It is not natural for a Spirit-filled child of God to walk around discouraged. This is an attack of Satan to put us on the sidelines.

DIVISION

Francis Frangipane says, "If there ever was a false doctrine that was so widespread, so accepted in the body of Christ, yet so contrary to the heart and teachings of Christ, it is the tradition of division within the Church" (www.fangipane.org, "Becoming the Answer to Christ's Prayer" p. 2).

One of the most effective strategies of Satan has been to bring about division in the body of Christ. It makes sense that the enemy would push for a splintered, divided church, since Jesus desired exactly the opposite. The main focus of Jesus' great high priestly prayer of John 17 was that His followers would be united. A strong, united church is a testimony to the world of the love of God. Satan is doing all he can to destroy that testimony.

One of the main weapons we have against this attack is awareness of the enemy's schemes. If we are unaware of the satanic nature of division, there is a greater tendency toward excusing it or just assuming that this is one of those things that happens occasionally in the church. When we see clearly though, that we as a church are under attack, then we should determine at all costs to guard against division. The local congregation is well prepared to resist the enemy when, finding itself in times of conflict, each one begins to ask the question, "What is the enemy trying to do here?" Then, turning to the Lord, each asks the most important question, "Lord, how do

the devil goes to church

we counter the attacks of the enemy against your people?"

When a church finds itself facing issues that bring division, the prayer meeting is far more effective than the board meeting. Division always has a spiritual issue at its root and the enemy is always involved. It is heart-felt, heaven-sent prayer by the body of Christ that will rout the devil and deal with the issues that are at hand.

I'll never forget a church in central Indiana where I taught a prayer seminar. I'm so grateful I got there early that Sunday morning. As I walked into the church sanctuary, I was amazed to see about a dozen men walking around the room praying. They were laying hands on the pews and walking to the four corners of the room, praying for a new awareness of the Lord's presence, a fresh moving of His Spirit, and for protection from the attacks of the enemy. What a powerful way for a group of Christian leaders to go on the offensive against Satan and to keep the devil from their local congregation.

keeping our spiritual armor ready for warfare

1. Do you agree with the statement, "the devil spends more time in church than many Christians"? Describe ways that you have seen this to be true.

2. Have you ever thought of the church as C.S. Lewis described it: "spread out through all time and space and rooted in eternity, terrible as an army with banners"? What can we do to restore this grand vision of the church?

3. How is studying Scripture without doing what it says, a deception of Satan? What other areas of deception do you see in the church today?

4. Have you seen Christians who backed away from their church involvement because of discouragement? What can a local church do to help those who are discouraged?

5. What do you believe are the major reasons for division within a local congregation? How can a church protect itself against division?

the weapons of our warfare

"Like the Spartans, every Christian is born a warrior. It is his destiny to be assaulted, his duty to attack. Part of his life will be occupied with defensive warfare. He will have to defend the *faith once delivered to the saints*. He will have to resist the devil. He will have to *Stand against all the devil's wiles, and having done all, still to stand.* He will, however, be an ineffective Christian, if he acts only on the defensive. He must be one who goes against his foes, as well as [one who] stands still to receive their advance. He must be able to say with David, 'I come to thee in the Name of the Lord of Hosts. The God of the armies of Israel, whom thou has defied.' (I Sam. 17:45)."

C.H. Spurgeon

"The weapons we fight with are not the weapons of the world. On the contrary, they have divine power to demolish strongholds."
(2 Corinthians10:4)

We are in a war like no other. Because it is "spiritual" warfare, the weapons that we use cannot be the normal weapons of this world. The devil does not succumb to guns or bombs. Nor does he surrender to human wisdom or strategies.

Perhaps the best model of spiritual warfare in which spiritual weapons are used is that of Jesus and the temptations in the wilderness. Look carefully at how Jesus resisted the wiles of the devil:

> *Then Jesus was led by the Spirit into the desert to be tempted by the devil. After fasting forty days and forty nights, he was hungry. The tempter came to him and said, "If you are the Son of God, tell these stones to become bread."*
>
> *Jesus answered, "It is written: 'Man does not live on bread alone, but on every word that comes from the mouth of God.'"*
>
> *Then the devil took him to the holy city and had him stand on the highest point of the temple. "If you are the Son of God," he said, "throw yourself down. For it is written:*
>
> *'He will command his angels concerning you, and they will lift you up in their hands,*
>
> *so that you will not strike your foot against a stone.'"*
>
> *Jesus answered him, "It is also written: 'Do not put the Lord your God to the test.'"*
>
> *Again, the devil took him to a very high mountain and showed him all the kingdoms of the world and their splendor. "All this I will give you," he said, "if you will bow down and worship me."*
>
> *Jesus said to him, "Away from me, Satan! For it is written: 'Worship the Lord your God, and serve*

him only.'"

Then the devil left him, and angels came and attended him" (Matthew 4:1-11).

With every thrust of Satan's sword of lies, Jesus parried with the Sword of the Lord, God's Word. "It is written" is the trademark of every response of Jesus to the attack of the enemy. Even the Son of God did not leave spiritual warfare to His own strength of character or will, but instead fought the battle with the spiritual weapon of the Word of God. What a model this is for us in our daily battle! It has been said that we should know the Word of God so well that when we are asked our opinion on anything, we naturally give God's.

On a very practical level, this battle is won by the use of the Word of God and prayer. Prayer keeps us in communication with our Commander-in-Chief. As we pray, He directs us, guides us, protects us, and even shows us the parts of His Word that are needed for the victory at any given moment. Have you not experienced that quickening of His Spirit in which His Word comes to your mind at just the right time for just the right purpose?

I remember that as a child growing up in church we would have what we called "sword drills" in youth group. In contest form we would try to respond to questions our leaders asked us with the correct Bible verse as quickly as possible. Though as children we saw it as a game, in a very real sense, we were being trained for a very real war. It is an unfortunate soldier who must learn to use a weapon in the midst of battle. How much better it is to be trained in the proper use of your weapon in the relative safety and security of your comrades and in training camp.

When Scripture says, *"Do your best to present yourself to God as one approved, a workman who does not need to be ashamed and who correctly handles the word of truth"* (2 Timothy 2:15), it is a clear call for serious training in the use of the spiritual weapon of the Word.

> If you as a believer do not have a working knowledge of Scripture, you will likely become a casualty in this spiritual battle we are in. Remember, the best defense to warding off the attacks of the Temptor is a good offense. And there is just no better offense against the enemy known as "temptation" than the proper knowledge and use of the Word of God (Greg Laurie, *The Great Compromise.* Word, 1994, pp. 62-63).

While most Christians would agree to the value of studying and knowing God's Word, our failures typically come in the area of actually using the Word in warfare. This is where prayer comes in. We must learn to pray God's Word back to Him. Our spiritual weapons for defeating the enemy are the Bible and prayer.

Beth Moore, in her powerful book, *Praying God's Word,* explains this well:

> In Ephesians 6:10-18, Paul listed the whole armor of God. Only one piece of the armor is actually a weapon. The figurative belt, shield, breastplate, shoes, and helmet are all defensive pieces of armor intended to keep us from being injured by the weapons of the evil one. The sword of the Spirit, clearly identified as

the Word of God, is the only offensive weapon listed in the whole armor of God. Second Corinthians 10:3 uses the plural, assuring us we have weapons for warfare. What would the other primary weapon be? Perhaps additional weapons might be identified elsewhere, but I believe the other primary weapon of our warfare is stated right after the words identifying the sword of the Spirit as the Word of God in Ephesians 6:17. The next verse says, "And pray in the Spirit on all occasions." I am utterly convinced that the two major weapons with divine power in our warfare are the Word of God and Spirit-empowered prayer.

S.D. Gordon writes,

"The purpose of prayer is not to persuade or influence God, but to join forces with him against the enemy.

When we don't feel like praying is the moment we need to pray the most. Too often, we get in the middle of a mood swing and stay away from the presence of God because we don't feel like it. The devil wins.

"It is in Satan's best interest to keep the saints off their knees. Praying Christians are dangerous Christians. So Satan tries every trick in the book to keep us from staying in touch with God" (Cynthia Bezek, *PRAY!* Sept/Oct 1999 [Issue 14] pp. 22-25).

One of the key reasons for prayerlessness in the Christian life is a theological one. Deep inside, many Christians believe that prayer really doesn't matter. God is going to do whatever He is going to do and prayer isn't really going to change anything. If that is so . . . then why pray? Why spend time doing that which is ineffective for change?

The answer is that this is bad theology. The Bible clearly teaches that prayer not only changes the *person* that prays but also it changes *situations*. Scripture is filled with examples of people who prayed and, as a result, their situations changed. That is true on a personal scale such as a Hannah praying for a son, or on a national scale such as King Jehoshaphat praying for deliverance for Judah.

One of the best teaching sections on the power of prayer comes from the famous "gap" passage in Ezekiel 22:30:

> *"I looked for a man among them who would build up the wall and stand before me in the gap on behalf of the land so I would not have to destroy it, but I found none."*

This is an amazing verse that shows us the all-powerful, Creator of the universe, looking for someone to pray before He begins to act. The people of God, as a result of their sin and rebellion against God, were in a position in which their sins required punishment. In this case, the punishment was to be the destruction of the city of Jerusalem. Though this was the decreed punishment, our merciful God was willing to delay or even avert this catastrophe if there would be someone who would intercede before Him on Jerusalem's behalf; someone to "stand in the gap" so that God might not have to destroy the city. God looked for such a person, but could find no one. Prayer could have made a difference then. It still can today. God is waiting for His people to "stand before Him" on behalf of our land (2 Chronicles 7:14).

Why did Jesus pray? Was it simply to change Himself? Or did Jesus know that prayer was the way His Father had chosen to work on this planet? Jesus didn't waste time doing things just for religious show. Jesus prayed because prayer was His way of staying in touch with His Father and it demonstrated His dependency upon Him. When Jesus prayed, He expected God to act. His great High Priestly prayer in John 17 demonstrated that He expected the Father to do things in response, both in His prayers as well as the prayers of His disciples.

One of my favorite Bible stories that demonstrates how prayer changes things is found in Exodus 17. It is the story of how Israel defeated the Amalekites in the wilderness. After being attacked by the warlike Amalekites at Rephidim, Moses told Joshua to gather his men and go to war the next day. As for Moses, he would be standing at the top of a nearby hill where he could see the battle. This exciting story continues in Exodus:

> So Joshua fought the Amalekites as Moses had ordered, and Moses, Aaron and Hur went to the top of the hill. As long as Moses held up his hands, the Israelites were winning, but whenever he lowered his hands, the Amalekites were winning. When Moses' hands grew tired, they took a stone and put it under him and he sat on it. Aaron and Hur held his hands up—one on one side, one on the other—so that his hands remained steady till sunset. So Joshua overcame the Amalekite army with the sword (17:10-13).

Why would the position of an old man's hands have anything to do with the battle in the valley below? Lifted hands have always been a symbol of prayer. As long as God was involved through prayer, Israel won the victory. In Exodus 17:16, after the battle, Moses built an altar to the Lord and he said, *"For hands were lifted up to the throne of the LORD."* This was no idle spiritual calisthenics. It was an expression of the power of prayer to change situations.

One of the main reasons so many Christians fail to pray or believe the wrong things about prayer is the seeming "hit or miss" aspect to much of our praying. Sometimes it works, sometimes it doesn't. So we develop a bad theology to cover our misses and turn prayer into something it was never meant to be.

This problem happens when we look at prayer as a way of getting things from God. If I pray long enough, have enough faith, get enough people to join me in prayer, just maybe I'll get what I want from God. But prayer is not "my way of getting things from God." Prayer is God's chosen way of accomplishing His will on this planet! My job in prayer is to draw near in intimacy. As I begin to understand a bit of the Lord's heart on a matter, then I begin to ask Him to accomplish what is already His will. It is at that point that prayer becomes a powerful change agent to achieve the Lord's purposes.

In spiritual warfare, it is prayer that keeps us connected to our Commander-In-Chief. Consequently, prayer becomes strategic in warfare. It is prayer that gives us our supply line of provisions for the battle. It is prayer that unleashes the power of God's Word to accomplish its purpose in overcoming the enemy. John Piper said it this way, "Until we know that life is war, we won't know what prayer is for."

My wife and I often share with churches that the one

thing that has changed our individual prayer lives more than any other is learning to pray the Lord's Word back to Him. My favorite way to pray is, "open eyes, open Bible." As I read through the Bible, I'm led again and again to pray about that which is clearly God's will. I find myself praying about things I had never considered praying about, in ways I had never expected to pray.

All of us can do that. It doesn't require special training or aptitude. We simply open our Bibles and begin to pray about what we are reading. Sometimes it is a matter of asking the Lord to teach us, to give us understanding of His Word. Other times there are clear ways of praying the Word into our own lives or the lives of those around us.

Let me give you an example. When I travel to many churches, I am often asked to pray for local congregations. Now there are many things I could pray over a congregation that would be good. What I love to pray, though, is what I know God desires to bring about in that fellowship. So I turn to Ephesians 3:14 and begin praying in my own words, personalizing and applying Scripture to a particular group.

I kneel before You in prayer, Father, from whom our whole family in heaven and on earth derives our name. I pray that out of Your glorious riches You might strengthen this church with power through Your Spirit in their inner being, so that You, Lord Jesus, might dwell in their hearts through faith. I pray that the brothers and sisters here, being rooted and established in love, might have the power, together with all the saints, to grasp how wide and long and high and deep is Your love, O Christ. And that they might know this love that surpasses knowledge—that they might be filled to the measure of all Your fullness, Lord.

It is this sort of praying that overcomes the enemy! It is not based on my emotions or desires, but on the revealed truth of God's will in Scripture. It touches God's heart because it emerges from God's heart.

It is scriptural praying that allows us to resist the enemy, much as Jesus did in the wilderness temptations. Peter writes in 1 Peter 5:8:

"Be self-controlled and alert. [Why?] *Your enemy the devil prowls around like a roaring lion looking for someone to devour."*

In the previous chapter of 1 Peter we read in verse 7b:

"Therefore be clear minded and self-controlled so that you can pray."

In both verses self-control is commanded. Self-control is needed if we are to pray with power and passion. And prayer is needed if we are to be successful in resisting the devil.

1. What do you believe are our most effective weapons against Satan? How can your church do a better job in training Christians in the use of those weapons?

2. Jesus used the Word of God in His wilderness battle against Satan. On a practical level, how can you use the Word in spiritual warfare?

3. Is praying the Word a regular part of your life? Have you viewed this activity as warfare? How can it become a more effective weapon in your hands?

4. Does your church have members with a "bad theology" of prayer? Do you agree with the author's contention that "prayer is God's chosen way of accomplishing His will on this planet?" Why or why not?

5. Why do you believe Jesus prayed?

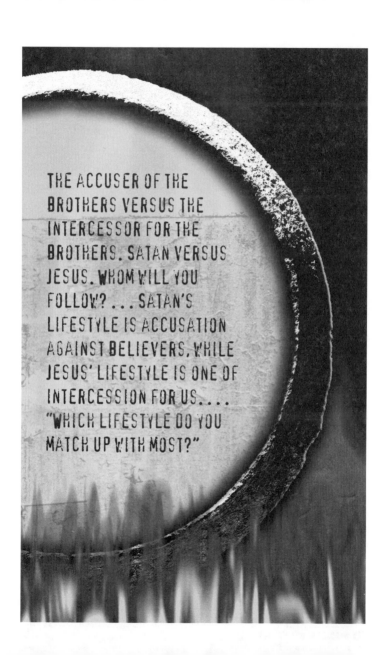

THE ACCUSER OF THE BROTHERS VERSUS THE INTERCESSOR FOR THE BROTHERS. SATAN VERSUS JESUS. WHOM WILL YOU FOLLOW? ... SATAN'S LIFESTYLE IS ACCUSATION AGAINST BELIEVERS, WHILE JESUS' LIFESTYLE IS ONE OF INTERCESSION FOR US.... "WHICH LIFESTYLE DO YOU MATCH UP WITH MOST?"

the intercessor vs. the accuser

We live in the midst of battle, in a time of spiritual intensity. Every word and action is important. It is a time of choices for us. Whom will we follow? How will we live? The opportunity for these choices occurs every day. Every time we open our mouths. Every time we choose to allow something into our thought processes.

The choice the Bible speaks of really is a choice between two people, representing two very different lifestyles. These two people and their lifestyles in the midst of the battle in this life are found in Revelation 12 and Hebrews 7. They are the accuser and the Intercessor.

And there was war in heaven. Michael and his angels fought against the dragon, and the dragon and his angels fought back. But he was not strong enough, and they lost their place in heaven. The great dragon was hurled down—that ancient serpent called the devil, or Satan, who leads the whole world astray. He was hurled to the earth, and his angels with him.

Then I heard a loud voice in heaven say:

"Now have come the salvation and the power

and the kingdom of our God,
and the authority of his Christ.
For the accuser of our brothers,
who accuses them before our God day and night,
has been hurled down.
They overcame him
by the blood of the Lamb
and by the word of their testimony;
they did not love their lives so much
as to shrink from death.
Therefore rejoice, you heavens
and you who dwell in them!
But woe to the earth and the sea,
because the devil has gone down to you!
He is filled with fury,
because he knows that his time is short."

(Revelation 12:7-12)

"Therefore he is able to save completely those who come to God through him, because he always lives to intercede for them."

(Hebrews 7:25)

The accuser of the brothers versus the Intercessor for the brothers. Satan versus Jesus. Whom will you follow? It's easy for us to jump up and say with indignation, "Why would you even hint at the possibility that I would follow Satan? I'm a Christian, a follower of Jesus!" I'm not interested here in labels, but in lifestyles. Satan's lifestyle is accusation against believers, while Jesus' lifestyle is one of intercession for us. My question is, "Which lifestyle do you match up with more?"

I see and hear of many churchgoers who seem to feel they have the spiritual gift of criticism. Accusing their fellow believers is pretty much a weekly event. Would it shock them to know they are doing the accuser's "ministry"? Our job is to pray for our brothers and sisters, not to criticize them. Intercession is what Jesus is doing.

Accusation comes so easily to us. We don't have to decide to be critical. The people around us do plenty of things that warrant criticism. We all carry around enough flaws to attract accusation. What is critical for us to see though, is that accusation is the job of Satan, not the job of the Christian. We're called to intercede, not accuse. This critical spirit has become so rampant in our churches that I felt it warranted an entire chapter to deal with it.

Francis Frangipane writes,

> Once, while driving home from a meeting, I realized that my mind was filled with arguments and criticism about the other spiritual leaders with whom I had met. It suddenly occurred to me that I didn't really intend to be critical or unloving toward these people. Yet my mind was overflowing with negative thoughts against my friends. I had to catch myself and recognize that these thoughts were from the enemy.
>
> The enemy loves to discredit people and destroy relationships. It is Satan's delight to fill our minds with accusations against our husbands or wives, our leaders, our friends, or people from a particular country or city, or against God himself. He is "the father of lies" (John 8:44) and the "accuser of our brethren" (Rev.12:10) (*The Three Battlegrounds,* p. 43).

Occasionally I'll hear someone say in response to this, "Well, I'm entitled to my opinion." Really? Says who? Where do you find that in Scripture? If you're a Christian, I find in the Bible that you have died to self. It is no longer you living, but Christ living in you. Has the Lord who lives in you given you special permission to accuse or criticize another one of His servants? This is serious, friends. It's a matter of warfare.

The critical spirit that is rampant in our churches is an indicator of the strength of the enemy within the church. He has deceived us into thinking that if someone has done something wrong, or even if we disagree with him, then it's okay to criticize him. That's especially true if the offender happens to be a Christian leader. Leaders seem to be easy marks for the critical spirit.

Pulpit ministers are dropping out of ministry in record numbers. One of the reasons given is the critical spirit that to always seems to be present, no matter what they do. Satan has always attacked leaders. Satan's assault on Job (see Job 1-2) involved first of all accusing this godly leader before God. Another lesser-known story involves the High Priest Joshua during the time of the prophet Zechariah. In Zechariah 3:1 we read, *"Then he showed me Joshua the high priest standing before the angel of the LORD, and Satan standing at his right side to accuse him."* Satan is still doing the same thing. The tragedy is that so many Christians allow themselves to be used by the enemy to achieve his aim of discrediting and discouraging Christian leaders.

Paul had a different approach of ministering to those in authority. Not through the ministry of accusation, but that of intercession. In 1 Timothy 2:1-4, he wrote,

"I urge then, first of all, that requests, prayers, intercession and thanksgiving be made for everyone—for kings and all those in authority, that we may live peaceful and quiet lives in all godliness and holiness. This is good and pleases God our Savior, who wants all men to be saved and to come to a knowledge of the truth."

The command of Scripture is to pray for those in authority. I would suggest that this is not only for civil authorities, but church leaders as well. It is especially interesting when you consider the horrible character and evil intent of the Roman emperors of Paul's day. Yet his command is to intercede for those leaders, even when they were not good rulers. How much more should we find ourselves then, interceding for our presidents and governors and mayors? Then consider the godly ministers among us who are serving God and us. Are they not in great need of our intercessions?

We need once again to try to understand Satan's schemes. He has some understanding of parts of Scripture. He certainly has grabbed hold of Zechariah 13:7 which warns, *"Strike the shepherd, and the sheep will be scattered. . . ."* In congregation after congregation, the accuser has come against pastors (shepherds) and the result has been a scattered flock. It is time for a militant church to stand against the lies and schemes of the enemy.

We have no perfect preachers. Our leaders lack. We can always find fault if we look. But God is calling us not to look for fault but to pray for those in authority (1 Timothy 2:1-4). In this way, we defeat Satan in a very practical way in our own local congregation. A prayed-for preacher is a loved and respected preacher who will be found more effective than ever before in his ministry because of the peoples' prayers.

1. Do you find that criticism comes naturally to you? Are there particular things that bring out criticism in you more than others?

2. Have you ever looked at criticism (accusation) as coming from Satan? Do you find that it's easier to think of criticism as evil when it comes from others rather than when it comes from you?

3. Do you believe there is a critical spirit within your church? What should church leaders do to combat this critical spirit?

4. Jesus has a current ministry of intercession. Do you have this ministry in your own life? How seriously do you take it when someone asks you to pray about a situation?

5. Do you agree that pastors are under attack? How can your church mobilize protective prayers for its leaders?

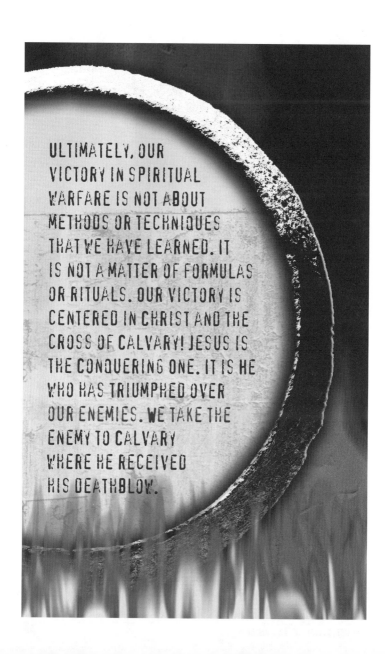

ULTIMATELY, OUR VICTORY IN SPIRITUAL WARFARE IS NOT ABOUT METHODS OR TECHNIQUES THAT WE HAVE LEARNED. IT IS NOT A MATTER OF FORMULAS OR RITUALS. OUR VICTORY IS CENTERED IN CHRIST AND THE CROSS OF CALVARY! JESUS IS THE CONQUERING ONE. IT IS HE WHO HAS TRIUMPHED OVER OUR ENEMIES. WE TAKE THE ENEMY TO CALVARY WHERE HE RECEIVED HIS DEATHBLOW.

the nature of our victory

"Victory begins with the name of Jesus on our lips.
It is consummated by the nature of Jesus in our heart."
(Francis Frangipane, *The Three Battlegrounds*, p. 34)

Dwight L. Moody told a story of a young man that he knew who took a serious fall while still young and became paralyzed from the waist down. He was in very real pain every day of his life and was confined to bed. Yet Moody said that when he visited this young man's room, it was as though he entered heaven itself. The man was so overflowing with the love of God and so grateful for what God had done for him.

Moody commented to him about this apparent awareness of the presence of God and asked him whether or not he was ever tempted to fall into discouragement.

"Oh yes," the young man responded, "many times. I will be laying here looking out my window and I see people my age walking about and enjoying life in fullness of health and the devil begins to whisper to me, "If God loved you, why did he allow this to happen to you."

"What do you do then?" said Moody.

"Ah," he responded, "I just take the devil to Calvary and show him Jesus' hands and feet and side. And then I say, 'Doesn't he love me?' And the truth is, Satan got such a scare there two thousand years ago that he leaves me every time."

OUR VICTORY CENTERED IN CHRIST

Ultimately, our victory in spiritual warfare is not about methods or techniques that we have learned. It is not a matter of formulas or rituals. Our victory is centered in Christ and the cross of Calvary! Jesus is the Conquering One. It is He who has triumphed over our enemies. We take the enemy to Calvary where he receives his deathblow.

In Psalm 44, we see a great picture of the power of Jesus to overcome the enemy. It is a wonderfully balanced view, showing that the power for victory is in the Lord, but that we must wield the weapons and walk in obedience to the directions of God.

> You are my King and my God,
> who decrees victories for Jacob.
> Through you we push back our enemies;
> through your name we trample our foes.
> I do not trust in my bow,
> my sword does not bring me victory;
> but you give us victory over our enemies,
> you put our adversaries to shame.
> In God we make our boast all day long,
> and we will praise your name forever.

(Psalm 44:4-8)

the nature of our victory

Notice the emphasis on the *Lord's* role in this victory:

- "Through YOU we push back our enemies"
- "Through YOUR name"
- "YOU give us victory"
- "YOU put our adversaries to shame"

> *"See, the Lion of the tribe of Judah,*
> *the Root of David, has triumphed."*
>
> (Revelation 5:5b)

Daily victory in spiritual warfare is always all about Jesus. It is in keeping our eyes on Jesus that we walk as those who are "more than conquerors." Overcoming the darkness is much more about allowing the light of Christ to shine through us than about shouting at the darkness.

Though spiritual warfare is a reality that cannot be avoided, the real value of studying this issue is that it drives us to Jesus. As we understand more of our enemy and his schemes, we find ourselves running to Jesus, our Fortress and Protector.

We have a God who is so much more powerful than Satan that He really can't defeat Satan. Now bear with me. Listen. Satan is a created being and as such is far below God in power and authority. Satan is too small and God is simply too big for there to be any contest at all.

To help us understand, let's use our imaginations for a minute. Suppose that a cocky little ant comes up to you one day and challenges you to an arm-wrestling contest. Now you really can't do that. You can't win at arm-wrestling with this tiny ant. You're too big and the ant is too small. You could move your thumb over and crush it . . . but you can't beat it at arm-wrestling because of the disparity of size. Unless of course, you became an ant. And as an ant, you could engage that challenger and defeat it.

Which is exactly what our Creator God did in the incarnation. Creator took on human flesh. The unimaginably Big became unbelievably Small. And as a man, God took on the enemy of our souls, the great Dragon, Satan and defeated him on a cross 2,000 years ago. That is our victory.

OUR LIFE BETWEEN THE "ALREADY" AND THE "NOT YET"

Christians today live in an interesting and challenging time, both practically and theologically. We live in the already and the not yet. There are certain aspects of the Christian life that are "already" secured for us. God has already done everything needed to provide for our salvation. Still, there is the "not yet" aspect in which we are still *"working out our salvation."* In a very real way, our warfare is also a part of the "already" and the "not yet."

Our victory is assured. Jesus has won the victory. I often hear believers talk about how they have read the end of the book and we win. That's true. The Book of Revelation especially is about the overcoming Christ. But the assurance of victory does not make our current warfare any less harrowing or real. *This is a real fight.* People are killed daily in this war. Jesus called Satan a murderer and we need to understand that Satan is doing that today.

Using World War II as an illustration, it has been noted before that Christians today are living in that period between D-Day and VE (Victory in Europe) Day. On D-Day and the days that followed, the fate of the Axis powers was determined. Fortress Europe, as the Germans referred to it, had fallen to the allied invasion. Military strategists understood that it was just a matter of time until the final defeat of Nazi Germany. But during the nine months of fighting after D-Day, allied forces lost many thousands of men in battle. Assurance of victory doesn't mean the fighting is over.

Our Lord Jesus has triumphed over the enemy! Victory is ours. But the battle continues unabated. If anything, it appears that the church may be going through an even more intensive time of struggle. It has been noted that there is nothing more dangerous than a wounded lion. Satan, that wounded lion, is still on the prowl and the church ignores spiritual warfare at her own peril. The warning from Revelation 12:12 must be heeded:

> ". . . woe to the earth and the sea, because the devil has gone down to you! He is filled with fury, because he knows that his time is short."

That phrase, "his time is short" goes well with the passage in 1 Peter 4:7,

> "The end of all things is near. Therefore be clear minded and self-controlled so that you can pray."

Perhaps the greatest need of our day is for praying Christians. When we look at the warfare, both in the world and in the church, the clear-minded, self-controlled Christian will drop to his or her knees in fervent, Spirit-led prayer. The church triumphant is a church connected with her Head through prayer and moving boldly through the current warfare with her eyes fixed firmly on Jesus.

". . . take heart! I have overcome the world."
(John 16:33)
Jesus

1. In the midst of life's struggles, how easy or difficult is it to believe that the war is already won? How can we make this truth an active part of our lives?

2. Scripture tells us to fix our eyes on Jesus. How do you do that in your daily experience? Is it something that can be taught?

3. How do you feel about the statement that God is too big and powerful to defeat Satan? Did the author's explanation make sense to you?

4. Do you believe that spiritual warfare is a real battle in which people are getting killed? Have you had a tendency to view spiritual warfare as simply an interesting way of looking at things rather than reality?

5. What do you see going on in our world today that is an indicator that the enemy is "filled with fury" and actively doing harm? How do you see the church going on the counter-attack?

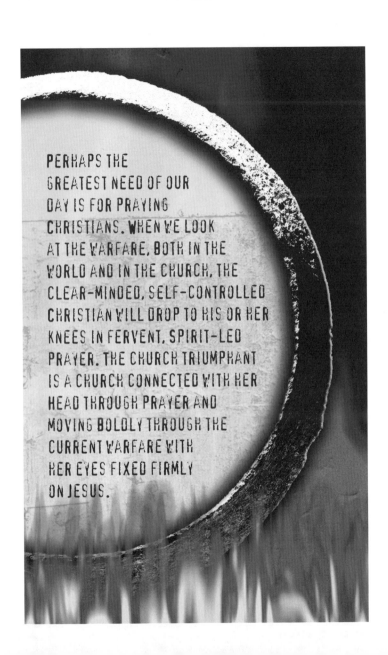

PERHAPS THE GREATEST NEED OF OUR DAY IS FOR PRAYING CHRISTIANS. WHEN WE LOOK AT THE WARFARE, BOTH IN THE WORLD AND IN THE CHURCH, THE CLEAR-MINDED, SELF-CONTROLLED CHRISTIAN WILL DROP TO HIS OR HER KNEES IN FERVENT, SPIRIT-LED PRAYER. THE CHURCH TRIUMPHANT IS A CHURCH CONNECTED WITH HER HEAD THROUGH PRAYER AND MOVING BOLDLY THROUGH THE CURRENT WARFARE WITH HER EYES FIXED FIRMLY ON JESUS.

- Anderson, Neil T. *Victory over the Darkness: Realizing the Power of Your Identity in Christ.* Ventura, CA: Regal Books, 1990.

- ———. *The Bondage Breaker.* Eugene, OR: Harvest House, 1990.

- Anderson, Neil T., and Timothy M. Warner. *The Beginner's Guide to Spiritual Warfare.* Ann Arbor, MI: Servant Publications, 2000.

- Arnold, Clinton E. *Powers of Darkness: Principalities and Powers in Paul's Letters.* Downers Grove, IL: InterVarsity Press, 1992.

- Bubeck, Mark. *The Adversary.* Chicago: Moody, 1975.

- ———. *Overcoming the Adversary.* Chicago: Moody, 1984.

- Dawson, John. *Taking Our Cities for God: How to Break Spiritual Strongholds.* Lake Mary, FL: Creation House, 1989.

- Dickason, C. Fred. *Demon Possession and the Christian: A New Perspective.* Westchester, IL: Crossway, 1987.

- Frangipane, Francis. *The Three Battlegrounds.* Robins, IA Advancing Church Publications, 1989.

- Kraft, Charles H. *Christianity with Power: Your Worldview and Your Experience of the Supernatural.* Ann Arbor: Vine Books, 1989.

- Lewis, C.S. *The Screwtape Letters.* 1942. Reprint. New York, NY: HarperCollins, 2001.

- Murphy, Ed. *The Handbook of Spiritual Warfare.* Nashville: Nelson, 1992.

- Penn-Lewis, Jessie. *War on the Saints.* New York: Thomas E. Lowe, 1973.

- Sherman, Dean. *Spiritual Warfare for Every Christian.* Seattle: Frontline, 1990.

- Wagner, C. Peter. *Prayer Shield.* Ventura, CA: Regal, 1992.

- Warner, Timothy M. *Spiritual Warfare.* Wheaton, IL: Crossway, 1991.

- White, Tom. *Breaking Strongholds: How Spiritual Warfare Sets Captives Free.* Ann Arbor, MI: Servant Publications, 1993.

- ———. *The Believer's Guide to Spiritual Warfare.* Ann Arbor, MI: Servant Publications, 1990.

Dave Butts is founder and President of Harvest Prayer Ministries. He serves as Chairman of America's National Prayer Committee and President of Gospel Revivals, Inc., publishers of *Herald of His Coming*. Dave also contributed the "Fasting" chapter in *The Preachers' Teacher: the Meaning and Message of the Sermon on the Mount* also published by Covenant Publishing.

He is married to Kim, and together they have two sons, Ron and David.

Harvest Prayer
MINISTRIES

BRINGING THE PRAYER MOVEMENT TO YOUR CHURCH

OUR MISSION

To call and equip the church to become a House of Prayer for all nations, in order to see revival and the finishing of the task of world evangelization.

OFFERING

• Leadership Seminars •

• Prayer Conferences •

• On-Site Consultation to help a local church •

• Retreat Center for Christian Leaders •

• Videos, Tapes, Books and other great resources
to help your church grow in prayer •

• Web Site •

FOR MORE INFORMATION • www.harvestprayer.com

or contact us at
Harvest Prayer Ministries
619 Washington Ave. • Terre Haute, IN 47802
(812) 238-5504

Founded in 1993 by Dave and Kim Butts